THE LAW OF ATTRACTION

INTRODUCTION

If you have taken the time to obtain this book, you are most likely wanting to change something about your appearance (or are simply a very curious person). There are many ways to change your looks, from getting a haircut to buying new make-up. This book will touch gently on these methods, but will focus largely on the power of changing your appearance with your thoughts. A brief introduction to The Law of Attraction will be given for those not familiar with the concept, as well as actionable tips to help you harness the power of your mind to create the changes you desire. While this book focuses on changing your physical appearance, these concepts can be applied to any area of your life.

THE LAW OF ATTRACTION

So, what is 'The Law of Attraction'? Wikipedia defines it as: "the name given to the belief that 'like attracts like' and that by focusing on positive or negative thoughts, one can bring about positive or negative results." And that really does sum-up the concept, but is a bit too high-level to be useful. The idea that 'like attracts like' is just that- that you draw to you experiences and objects that reflect your dominant mode of thought. If you are perpetually happy, optimistic, enthusiastic...you probably find that good things are constantly happening to you. After all, you go looking for positive experiences and outcomes, and they seem to magically appear! The same thing goes if your dominant mindset is a negative one: if you are constantly complaining about how bad everything is....why would you be surprised when more bad news shows up, you are pulling it to you like a magnet. The thoughts you think act as a broadcast signal that tells the universe what you would like to experience. One of the overarching themes of the law of attraction is that you get what you think of most, and the universe is always delivering what you are asking for. The problem is, often we are thinking about (and thus asking for) are things we don't want!

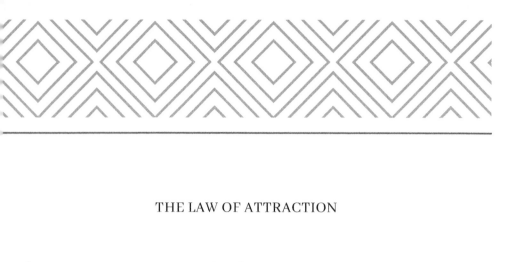

THE LAW OF ATTRACTION

There is a saying among people who espouse this belief that 'you don't get what you want, you get what you 'are'. You may desperately want a million dollars (who doesn't) but if the vast majority of your thoughts reflect a concern over a lack of money, and a general belief that you will never experience wealth, well then, you won't. After all, you've been 'asking' for lack, and the universe has delivered! This concept is applicable to our physical appearances- how many times are we negative in our self-talk? We desperately want thinner thighs, or a smaller or nose, or whatever the case may be. To use the example of wanting a smaller nose, if all you ever focus on is how large your nose is, the chance of it becoming smaller is slim (tee hee). So, how to go about changing your appearance with the law of attraction? If you want to change your looks, you must first change your mind.

I'LL SEE IT WHEN I BELIEVE IT

Can we really change our physical reality with just our mind alone? The answer is most definitely yes. Perhaps you have experienced this phenomenon yourself? Maybe you were a child and you wished for something and had it materialize? Or perhaps you visualized playing yourself playing sports or a taking test and found the outcome mirrored your expectations? There is plenty of evidence that indicates that what we think and feel affects what it is that we experience.

Age in Reverse

In fact, our minds are so powerful that researchers have been able to document the effect that our perception has on our reality, including changes to our physical bodies. One study set out to examine whether or not individuals could 'convince' themselves that they were younger than their actual age. The experiment took place in 1979, and has become somewhat infamous. Researchers gathered a group of 75 year old men and sent them back in time- in their minds at least. Everything around them was from the 1950's- the furniture, magazines, photos etc.

The men were instructed to behave or 'act as if' (more on that later) they were living in 1959. They were to talk about the jobs they held then, world events and personal experiences that happened in 1959. The men were also given ID badges with pictures of themselves at 55. Before the study began the men were tested for physical strength, eyesight, memory, and physical characteristics that tend to go downhill as we age. When the men were tested after the study, most of them had improved in every category- including becoming more flexible. If you can reverse age in a short period of time, you can certainly influence your confidence and your appearance.

I'LL SEE IT WHEN I BELIEVE IT

Get Fit Effortlessly

Many of us have internalized the narratives that we are told about fitness and exercise. We count the number of calories going in, and obsess about the amount of calories we burn. Changing the way we think about exercise can have just as dramatic of an effect as actually exercising. The average hotel room attendant approached to participate in a short study was found to clean an average of fifteen rooms each day, with each room taking somewhere between twenty and thirty minutes to clean. When these individuals were asked if they exercised, they all answered that they did not, even though the work they completed met the daily recommendation for exercise. The hotel attendants were split into two groups and monitored for 4 weeks. One group was told that their work provided the recommended amount of daily exercise, while the other group was not told this. The group advised that their work met the daily exercise requirements lost weight, lost body fat, had changes indicated in their hip-to-waist ratios and had their systolic blood pressure drop. These changes occurred even though the hotel room attendants did not change their habits.

I'LL SEE IT WHEN I BELIEVE IT

Get Fit Effortlessly

Many of us have internalized the narratives that we are told about fitness and exercise. We count the number of calories going in, and obsess about the amount of calories we burn. Changing the way we think about exercise can have just as dramatic of an effect as actually exercising. The average hotel room attendant approached to participate in a short study was found to clean an average of fifteen rooms each day, with each room taking somewhere between twenty and thirty minutes to clean. When these individuals were asked if they exercised, they all answered that they did not, even though the work they completed met the daily recommendation for exercise. The hotel attendants were split into two groups and monitored for 4 weeks. One group was told that their work provided the recommended amount of daily exercise, while the other group was not told this. The group advised that their work met the daily exercise requirements lost weight, lost body fat, had changes indicated in their hip-to-waist ratios and had their systolic blood pressure drop. These changes occurred even though the hotel room attendants did not change their habits.

I'LL SEE IT WHEN I BELIEVE IT

Thinking vs. Doing

In much the same way that being told that you are exercising has the ability to change your physical being, the act of visualizing yourself exercising has a similar effect. A study conducted at the Cleveland Clinic Foundation by exercise psychologist Guang Yue compared two groups of people. One group would actually go to the gym, while the other group would exercise in their mind. The group that went to the gym had an increase in muscle mass of 30%, while the group that exercised mentally had an increase in muscle mass of 13.5%. Granted, those who actually attended the gym had better results, but a 13.5% increase in lean muscle mass attributed only to visualization is pretty good! Similarly, a study that looked at the brain patterns of weightlifters lifting hundreds of pounds compared them to lifters that only imagined themselves lifting weights. In some cases, the mental practices were almost as effective as physical practice, and both exercise and visualization were more effective than doing either alone.

ASK, BELIEVE, RECEIVE

So, how can we put the law of attraction to work to begin manifesting physical changes? There are 3 basic steps to The Law of Attraction.

1) Ask: clearly ask the universe for what you want
2) Believe: believe the universe is delivering what you want
3) Receive (allow): this is the most important (and difficult) step

It seems so simple! And if it were that easy, there would be no need for this book to be written. However, the 'believe' and 'allow' steps can be a bit trickier than they initially seem. The believe part of the equation can be very difficult, especially if constantly confronted by your current reality. This can raise doubts about when, or if, you will be able to change your appearance. These doubts are commonly referred to as 'resistance'. Resistance can also block us during the receiving step, as this is where you need to be in emotional alignment with what you've asked for in order for your 'ask' to manifest.

ASK, BELIEVE, RECEIVE

Resistance usually takes the form of subconscious fears and doubts. Often times, we don't even realize they're there. They just anchor us to our current realities and prevent our desires from manifesting. They act as counter-intentions and the more attention and energy these fears are given, the father we move away from what we want. It isn't that the Law of Attraction isn't working. It's just that the universe is getting two different intentions to work on – what you want and what your fear. Wherever you focus the most energy upon is what the Law of Attraction will create. Ignoring fears and doubts rarely works because they linger in the background. If you want success with the Law of Attraction, resistance must be overcome.

IDENTIFYING RESISTANCE

And the first part of overcoming resistance? Well, identifying it for one, and trying to hone which ideas or behaviours are most responsible for keeping you from manifesting your desires. Imagine for a moment that your greatest dream has come true. What are the negative side effects, if any, from manifesting this dream? What are all of the different ways your life will change? Perhaps you want to lose weight. So you think, "what resistance could there possibly be to this desire, I want it so badly"....We will touch on 'wanting' later, though there may be more to the goal of weight loss than meets the eye. Is not losing weight acting as a coping mechanism, or an excuse for not doing things that make you feel uncomfortable? Maybe you told yourself that you would join that public speaking group....after you lost weight. Or that you would get on a dating site.... after you lost weight. We may think we want something and yet paradoxically block it if it keeps us in our comfort zone. Change, even change for the better, can be difficult.
.

IDENTIFYING RESISTANCE

There's no need to beat yourself up. Often, when we set an intention with our conscious mind, it is our subconscious mind that notices all the different ways things might change. Because we keep the awareness of the unintended outcomes at a subconscious level, we never deal with them at the conscious level. We try to think about our goal, and to feel great about it so as to match the vibration of what we want, but it is difficult to feel good and truly have faith when doubt and fear keeps popping up.

The reason this affects your results with the Law of Attraction so powerfully is because the Law of Attraction can only deliver situations and experiences that align with your dominant focus. If you have a bunch of counter-intentions clogging up your energetic "signal", you are essentially telling the universe, "Please send me more of this aggravation." Perhaps you spend 30 minutes a day visualizing the physical changes you wish to attract. During those 30 minutes, you are a deliberate creator! Your energetic "signal" to the universe is broadcasting exactly what you want, and you begin to draw it to you. However, if you spend the rest of each day feeling stressed by about life, your job, your body... you cannot allow for the blessings you desire to come into your life! Your focus on lack makes you incompatible with what you wish to manifest trying to attract. It doesn't mean you can't or won't make progress, but it will be slow and sporadic.

CATCH 22

"There was only one catch and that was Catch-22, which specified that a concern for one's safety in the face of dangers that were real and immediate was the process of a rational mind. Orr was crazy and could be grounded. All he had to do was ask; and as soon as he did, he would no longer be crazy and would have to fly more missions. Orr would be crazy to fly more missions and sane if he didn't, but if he were sane he had to fly them. If he flew them he was crazy and didn't have to, but if he didn't want to he was sane and had to. Yossarian was moved very deeply by the absolute simplicity of this clause of Catch-22 and let out a respectful whistle."

- Catch 22, Joseph Heller

Strictly speaking, a "Catch-22" is a problematic situation in which the only solution is denied by something inherent in the situation itself. The term "Catch-22" can refer to a problem, or a no-win or an absurd situation.

.

CATCH 22

So, in order to get what we want, we have to not want it at all? As mentioned above, when we approach manifestation from a place of 'lack' and 'want' we separate ourselves from our desires. It sounds absurdist, and a bit of a catch 22. And in some ways, it is. When we desperately want something, we tend to focus on how we don't not have what we want, keeping it at an increasing distance. We come to long for it more, and for our efforts we are awarded more longing. The key is a light touch. To want something without attaching many of the negative emotions we come to associate with want. Children are a great example of this. They are told to write a letter to Santa, and that he will deliver what they ask for on Christmas. So, they write their letters, send them off, and without really questioning the logistics of how Santa visits every house, even houses without chimneys, all on one night.....they expect their present to show up. They think about their new toys with joy and expectancy, not doubt and fear. And the analogy of expecting presents from Santa is apt, even for adults. The law of attraction encourages us dream and come to expect that the universe will deliver us our desires. The problem is, how do we get back to a state of joyful expectancy, when we wholeheartedly believed that we would receive what we have wished for, without creating blockages or resistance that separate us from our desires and their actualization?

.

CATCH 22

The receptive mode, also known as flow state or the vortex, is the primary mental and emotional state you'll want to hold when you're trying to manifest something specific. Being in receptive mode basically means that you are in the "zone", and feeling good as life unfolds. This is easier said than done, but there are several steps that can be taken that assist greatly in this process.

These exercises are just some of the ways that you can help to retrain your subconscious and conscious mind to help create the appearance you desire. The key is to tailor these tasks to your own needs so that you are having fun and enjoying the process.

.

YOU DON'T WANT WHAT YOU THINK YOU WANT

In many cases, you don't want what you think you want, or at least, not entirely. You may really want long hair, which is totally fine. But having longer hair is pretty arbitrary. There are plenty of beautiful hairstyles that are long, short and everything in between. The reason you want long hair is that you think you will feel better in the having of it- that you will feel more attractive, look better, feel more confident, whatever the case may be. You can be and feel those things regardless of your hair, and there are many ways of achieving those feelings; feelings of being beautiful, confident, attractive, that may not have anything to do with your hair. While you are waiting for your hair to catch up to your vision of your ideal-self, focus on all the other ways that you can feel the things you are hoping to feel when you hair grows out. Feeling those feelings now hastens the process by which you get to your desired future. If you can identify why it is that you want to change something about your appearance, you will be in a far better position to create work-arounds that will (paradoxically) help you achieve what you want.

.

DON'T WORRY ABOUT THE 'HOW'

Since you don't really want what you think you want, the universe
has room to get creative about how it delivers your results. You may
really want an extra thousand dollars to go on a trip. If the universe
delivered that trip as the prize to a contest you entered, instead of in
the format of a thousand dollars into your bank account, would that
really be so bad? Perhaps you really want to lose weight, or gain
some muscle mass but you cannot afford a gym membership. You
may feel that this is the only way you can get fit. But perhaps you will
be offered a job in landscaping, working outside all day, lifting plants
and dirt and doing very physical labour. Now you are getting paid to
work-out! The universe will deliver your results in the way it deems
the most efficient and appropriate for your situation.

.

RAISE YOUR VIBRATION

Ultimately, the key to successful manifesting is to raise your vibration. When resistance seems to distance us from the things we want, we are in a low vibrational energy. If you are nervous, tense, anxious, irritable, scared...this is a low vibration. When you start focusing on things that make you feel good, you shift your vibration. Your energy becomes focused on manifesting the things you want, and this speeds up the Law of Attraction. To get what you want, focus on feeling great. Listen to music you enjoy, watch a funny movie, get moving and start dancing. Whatever it is that makes you feel happy-spend time doing it.

A lot of time personal resistance consists of latent anxieties and stress. When we are stressed or worried, this can transfer to our manifesting process as stress is a killer of dreams.

 The best way to deliberate create your reality is to go with the flow. If you're not there yet, with a little bit of practice you can be! This book will provide just a few of the many ways to battle internal resistance.

.

THE FEELING IS THE SECRET

The Feeling is the Secret is a seminal work in the field of Law of Attraction that was written by Neville Goddard. Have you ever wanted something so much you could practically "taste it"? Perhaps it was a tangible item— such as a new shoes, a new car —or a desired experience –such as a new job or a wonderful vacation. Thinking about having these things just feels great. Without realizing it, you set in motion the Law of Attraction to bring this into your life. Unfortunately, most of the time our old training kicks in and we convince ourselves we'll never get what we want or we'd better plan on settling for something less instead. This can be why we often get things we don't really want, as we don't sabotage our manifesting with doubt and fear. We just think...."wouldn't it be nice to own those shoes", and they show up!

.If you want to change the kind of results your get in your life, the process starts with imagining how you wish to look and feeling amazing about it. From that mode of excitement, gratitude and rapture you will enter the 'receiving mode'—and begin attracting the "how to" steps to take next. People that can help you will show up in your life, special deals will suddenly pear. There will be all sorts of coincidences and signs that pop up while you are on your way to getting what you want.

THE FEELING IS THE SECRET

But it's not magic nor is it luck: it's using the power of our thoughts to magnetize to us the desired reality we wish to have. A great way to accomplish this is to start early. When you wake up every morning, your priority should be to start feeling good and get that momentum rolling. Decide that for today, you're not going to worry about the how. Decide that today you're going with the flow, and know that the Universe has planted all kinds of surprises, just to delight you. Resolve to care more about how you feel than about what you think of your situation. If you want to experience weight loss, but you are constantly focused on how 'fat' you are, you will receive more....fat. And you will not be in the receptive mode. So, in order to receive 'thin' you must think thin, or at least, think of your body in a way that expresses love and gratitude. By focusing on loving your body, you will receive a body that you love, and a self-reinforcing positive feedback loop will be triggered.

THE FEELING IS THE SECRET

But it's not magic nor is it luck: it's using the power of our thoughts to magnetize to us the desired reality we wish to have. A great way to accomplish this is to start early. When you wake up every morning, your priority should be to start feeling good and get that momentum rolling. Decide that for today, you're not going to worry about the how. Decide that today you're going with the flow, and know that the Universe has planted all kinds of surprises, just to delight you. Resolve to care more about how you feel than about what you think of your situation. If you want to experience weight loss, but you are constantly focused on how 'fat' you are, you will receive more....fat. And you will not be in the receptive mode. So, in order to receive 'thin' you must think thin, or at least, think of your body in a way that expresses love and gratitude. By focusing on loving your body, you will receive a body that you love, and a self-reinforcing positive feedback loop will be triggered.

DELIBERATE CREATION

"I understand there's a guy inside me who wants to lay in bed, smoke weed all day, and watch cartoons and old movies. My whole life is a series of stratagems to avoid, and outwit, that guy."

-Anthony Bourdain

ACTIONABLE STRATEGIES

There is a little saboteur that lives inside most of us that constantly undermines our desires for, and steps taken towards positive change. The nagging voice that tells us that we are not good enough, the limiting beliefs we have internalized from society, the difficulty in remaining positive when all we can focus on is 'what is'...Luckily, there are a number of stratagems to avoid, and outwit our resistance, so that we can experience the results we are looking for when. This twenty-one day experiment is designed to help you re-frame your thinking and improve your ability to manifest physical changes into your life. Hopefully by now you have a better understanding of The Law of Attraction, so without further ado, let's begin!

DAY ONE

One of the first steps you can take towards manifesting your goals is to take the pressure off. A big component of successful manifestation is to believe that you will receive the outcome you desire. If you wanted to manifest more money into your life because money was very tight, would you believe that you could manifest 5 million dollars in the next month? You would probably want to believe that you'd believe, but it is a bit of a stretch goal to say the least. It would be a lot easier to start with an extra 50 dollars in the first week. Once you've successfully manifested an extra 50 dollars, it will be much easier to believe that you can do 100 dollars the next week. And it is the same with our physical appearance. If you've managed to lose 1 pound in a week, 2 becomes more believable. As your success builds, so will your confidence in the process, and this allows you to ask for bigger things, in less time. Expecting your hair to grow ten inches in a month is just to much cognitive dissonance to be overcome on your first try. Remember, there's no pressure in successful manifestations- ever. Have fun with it!

EXERCISES FOR DAY ONE

Your task for the first day of this experiment is to identify one thing that would like to change about your appearance. If there isn't anything, that is fantastic! You can still benefit from this book by improving upon self-love and increasing confidence. However, if you are reading this you might have one or two attributes you wish you could improve upon.... Write down one of them in this notebook or in a digital document. This will be what you work on manifesting for the next 21 days. You will be adding to it throughout the course of this experiment.

MY LAW OF ATTRACTION GOAL

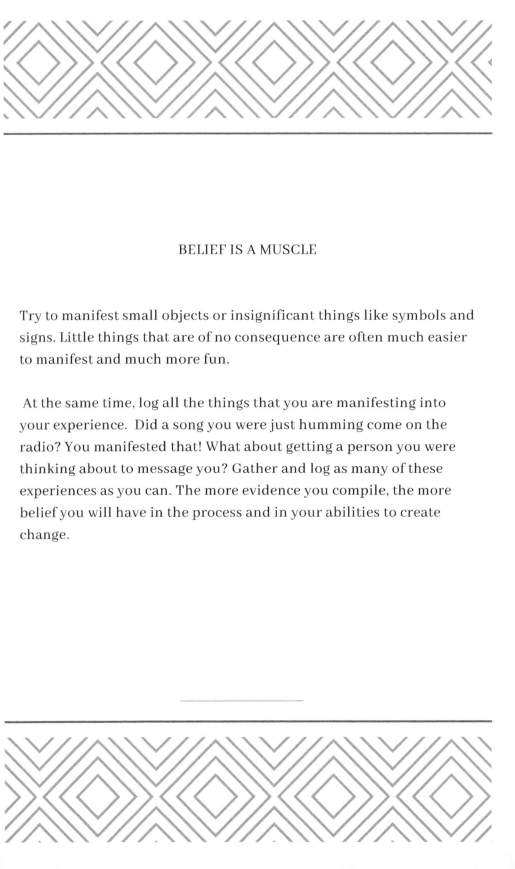

BELIEF IS A MUSCLE

Try to manifest small objects or insignificant things like symbols and signs. Little things that are of no consequence are often much easier to manifest and much more fun.

At the same time, log all the things that you are manifesting into your experience. Did a song you were just humming come on the radio? You manifested that! What about getting a person you were thinking about to message you? Gather and log as many of these experiences as you can. The more evidence you compile, the more belief you will have in the process and in your abilities to create change.

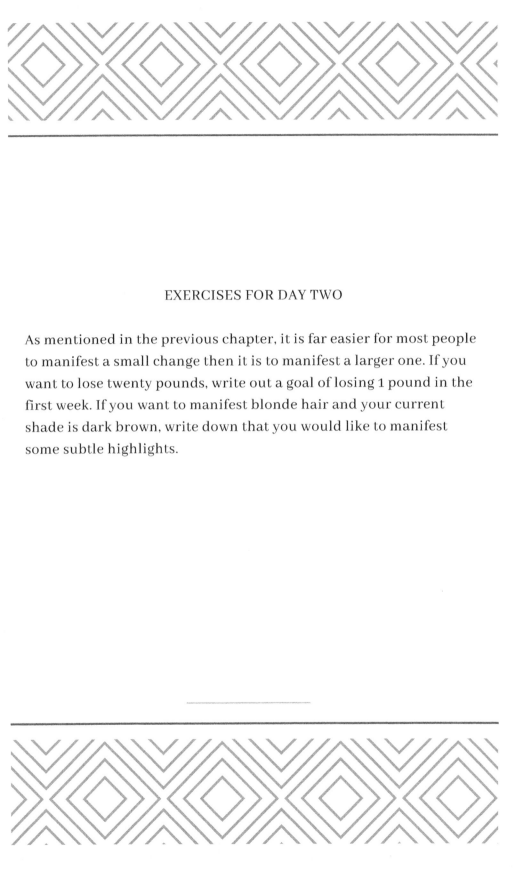

EXERCISES FOR DAY TWO

As mentioned in the previous chapter, it is far easier for most people to manifest a small change then it is to manifest a larger one. If you want to lose twenty pounds, write out a goal of losing 1 pound in the first week. If you want to manifest blonde hair and your current shade is dark brown, write down that you would like to manifest some subtle highlights.

MY FIRST GOALS

EMBRACE YOUR CURRENT STATE

Of course, this is easier said than done. Staring into a mirror and saying "I love my perfect body" when you clearly don't feel that way is not going to convince your subconscious mind, let alone your conscious mind that this is your new reality. Abraham/Ester Hicks have a great exercise where they ask people to create statements that lean towards their end goal while being believable in the moment. You will start with affirmations and beliefs that you currently accept, and keep increasing what you believe in the direction of your goal until you firmly believe that your body is perfect as is. You may wish to start with something as simple as "every healthy choice I make will move me closer to my goal". Or "I am proud of myself for taking action towards my goal".

It is also helpful to reinterpret negative thoughts. When you notice negative thoughts, transform them into positive thoughts. This will overcome resistance by shifting you to a higher vibrational level. For example, perhaps you're afraid that your friends will secretly disapprove of you losing weight.

EMBRACE YOUR CURRENT STATE

There is no need o pretend that change isn't scary. Maybe you are afraid that you will no longer be like your friends and that they will disapprove somehow. You cannot please everybody, and you may be surprised at how people come around, or were always planning on being supportive in the first place!

For this reason, carry out your experiment in secret. In "It Works: The Famous Little Red Book That Makes Your Dreams Come True!" there are five manifestation steps listed for manifesting your desires. Having only 5 steps is a pretty concise process- and "tell no one' made the cut. The reason this is so important is that other people, even other well-intentioned people can spur doubts and diminish your faith in the process. They may not mean to, but if you tell them that you are going to journal your way to longer hair...they may simply find this ridiculous. You may feel embarrassed to have even brought it up, or may begin to doubt why you even started the whole process anyway. If you have like-minded friends who improve your belief in The Law of Attraction, go ahead and mention your journey. If not, it is best to work in secret- they'll find out soon enough when you have manifested your desires.

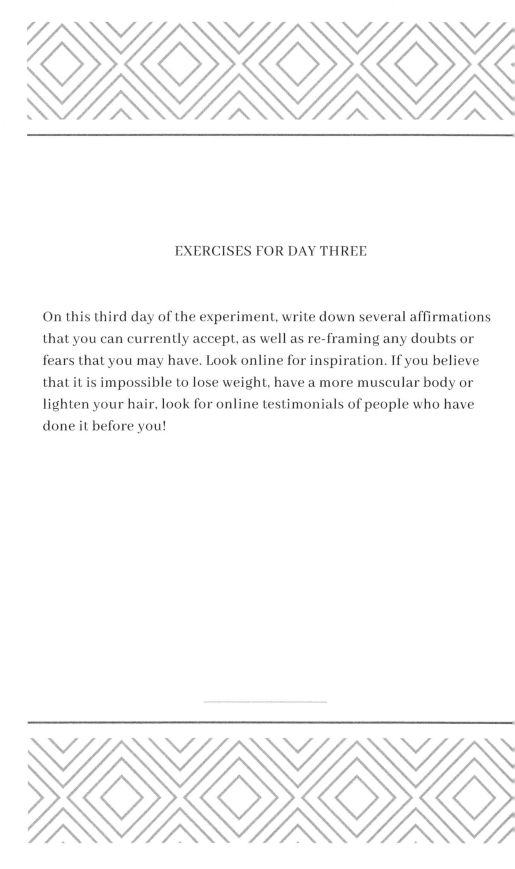

EXERCISES FOR DAY THREE

On this third day of the experiment, write down several affirmations that you can currently accept, as well as re-framing any doubts or fears that you may have. Look online for inspiration. If you believe that it is impossible to lose weight, have a more muscular body or lighten your hair, look for online testimonials of people who have done it before you!

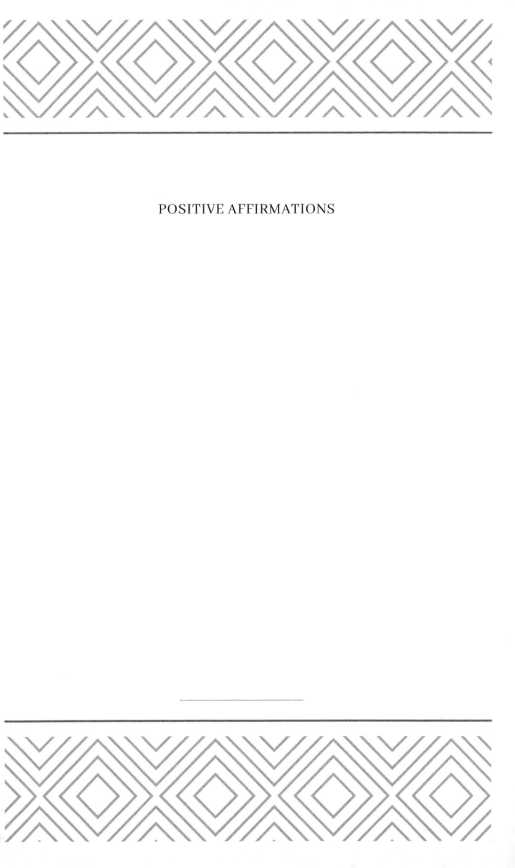

POSITIVE AFFIRMATIONS

TAKE ACTION

Now I know what you might be thinking.....that you're supposed to change your looks with your mind! Taking action to change your looks is hardly harnessing the power of The Law of Attraction. And that is true...to some extent. The point of taking action is not to slog away tirelessly and 'force' anything to happen. But action has a powerful effect both on your energy and on your mindset. Let's again use the example of a brunette that wants blonde hair. You could simply go out and bleach your hair blonde- there is no need to use The Law of Attraction. But let's say that you don't want to spend the money, don't want to damage your hair, don't want to risk it not turning out as you'd hoped etc. Could you use The Law of Attraction to manifest your desired hair colour? If you can think yourself young, I do not see why you cannot think yourself blonde. The key is of course to set targets that you actually believe are achievable. You may well be able to think yourself blonde; it may be a lot harder to think yourself into having vivid blue hair. But taking action towards a believable goal will help significantly. A quick Google of "how to go blonde no bleach" or "how to go blonde naturally" will often state that lemon juice or chamomile can lighten dark hair.

TAKE ACTION

If you were to spray these on your hair daily, you would be able to convincingly tell yourself that 'everyday my hair gets a bit lighter' or 'everyday my hair is getting lighter.' These are believable statements that help you positively re-frame your desires, and affirm your belief that you will receive what you have wished for. They key is to find a solution that you believe in, and work this into your routine. If you want to clear up acne, a Google search of 'vitamin A' should have you convinced that getting an adequate amount of vitamin A will improve your complexion. Please make sure that these actions are safe, however. It is important not to look too closely into a 'solution' so that you remain convinced, but it is also important not to gamble with your health!

EXERCISES FOR DAY FOUR AND FIVE

We are now on the 4th day of this experiment, and hopefully you are feeling far more confident about your ability to manifest change. Today's task is to come up with an actionable plan, perhaps one you discovered from yesterday's testimonials. Whatever action it is, write it down in your journal. Your task for day 5 will be to obtain whatever products you will require to put your plan into action. For the next 16 days, do whatever it is that will move you closer to your goal and shift your beliefs. You only have to take action until your new mindset takes hold.....

MY ACTION PLAN

WE ARE WHAT WE PRETEND TO BE

"We are what we pretend to be, so we must be careful about what we pretend to be."

— Kurt Vonnegut, Mother Night

"Acting as if' is a popular method for improving manifestation skills, and is mentioned quite often when the Law of Attraction is discussed. The concept is quite simple and is much akin to the old phrase "dress for the job you want, not the job you have." Perhaps you've heard the expression "fake it till you make it?" This concept is not new, nor is it by any means confined to Law of Attraction circles. The idea is that if you act as though you are already the person you wish to be, you will naturally become it.

In his book The Power of Awareness, Neville Goddard points out: "If you do not believe that you are He (the person you want to be), then you remain as you are. Through the faithful systematic cultivation of the feeling of the wish fulfilled, desire becomes the promise of its own fulfillment. The assumption of the feeling of the wish fulfilled makes the future dream a present fact." This act of pretending helps to convince your mind that you have in fact already received your desires, which helps to actualize your thoughts.

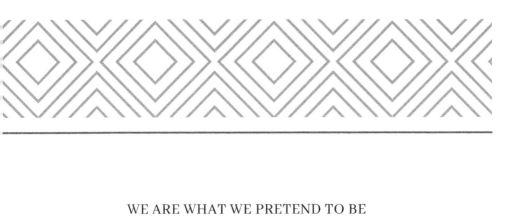

WE ARE WHAT WE PRETEND TO BE

"

"Acting as if" tailors nicely into taking action, although they are distinct. Let's say you wish to have bigger arm muscles. Why do you wish this were the case? Is it to feel more confident when wearing t-shirts or being topless? Is it to have more confidence when asking for dates? If it is because you wish to wish to feel more confident, you do not need to wait for arm muscles to develop to achieve that. How would this fit version of you act? Would they wear different clothes or behave differently? Can you achieve the same desire immediately by doing something else, say, putting some product in your hair or wearing a nice shirt? Actions that help you envision being your ideal-self all move you towards the goal-line, even if they are not directly related. Perhaps you could learn to play guitar or take stand-up lessons.

EXERCISES FOR DAY SIX

"Your task for day 6 is to write down a composite of how the person who has your desired characteristic would act. If you want longer hair, how would a person with very long hair behave? Undoubtedly they would take good care of their hair and likely keep it neat and styled. Incorporate 'acting as if' into your action plan from the previous day and be sure to act out this role. This is who you will be for the next fifteen days (and for the rest of time, once you become who you pretend you are).

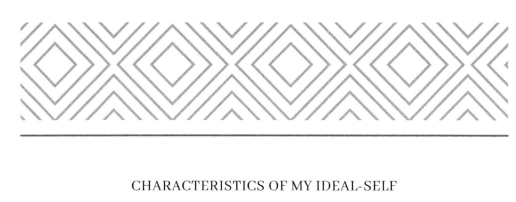

CHARACTERISTICS OF MY IDEAL-SELF

"

YOU WOKE UP WORTHY

"Feeling worthy of receiving what you have asked for is a huge part of seeing your desires actualize. Feeling worthy ties in well with taking action, as many of us do not believe that we can 'get something for nothing'. We have been told that everything in life is the result of hard work and perseverance. And certainly there is something to be said for hard work. The Law of Attraction doesn't run on hard work, nor is anything required on your part other than belief. But taking action can certainly help with the belief part, as we are then moving noticeably towards our goal, and taking a proactive role in the process can help us feel 'worthy' of what we desire. Feelings of unworthiness can creep in and can mess with our ability to believe we will receive whatever trait it is that we are asking for.

In much the same way that "Acting As If" does not have to pertain directly to what you are trying to manifest, increasing feelings of worthiness in any area will help to put you in a positive mindset and keep you in the receptive mode. Doing things consciously daily that make you feel good about yourself and increase your vibration will help in your manifestation.

YOU WOKE UP WORTHY

" These can be as simple or as elaborate as you wish, from picking up a piece of trash and placing it in the bin to doing volunteer work. Swap out your toothbrushes for biodegradable ones? Congratulate yourself, and think of this as increasing your personal stock so you can reap dividends on your efforts. Of course, the universe does not play tit-for-tat, but it is a great way to feel good while playing a little game to help increase your belief in the process.

EXERCISES FOR DAY SEVEN

Your task for day 7 is to write down all the reasons you are worthy. You can choose to draw from any area of your life. Perhaps you are a great teacher, or parent. You may volunteer, try to use environmentally friendly products. It does not matter how big or small the accomplishments are. Write down a list of things you do for yourself and others that are positive. In addition, write down several new things you can do to 'earn points' with the universe. You don't need to do anything to earn your desired appearance, but thinking of earning points is a fun game of increasing belief. Vow to pick up a piece of garbage on the sidewalk and put it in the trash this week. When you do, you are raising your vibration and can convince yourself that you are 'earning' your desires.

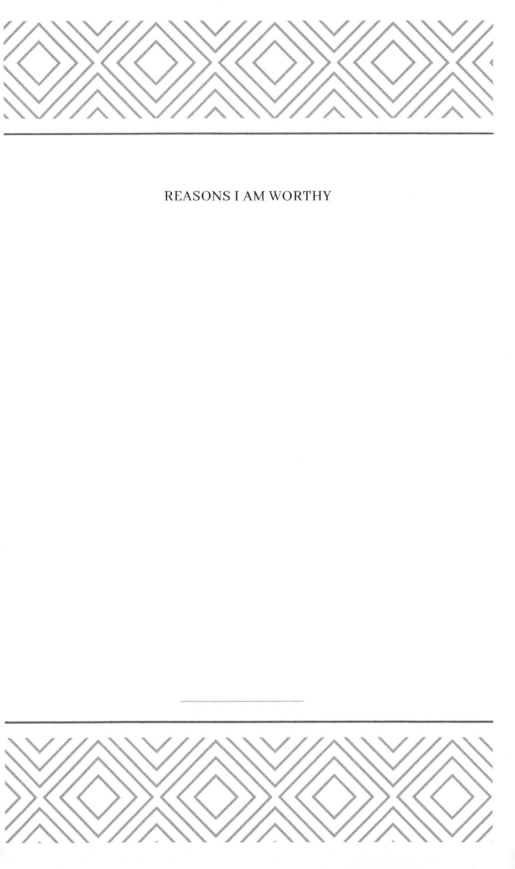

REASONS I AM WORTHY

IT IS DONE

Segment intending is a useful technique that Abraham/Ester Hicks speak of. Before you start any task, whether it is traveling somewhere, starting to clean, beginning a project....take a few moments to think about how you would like that experience to unfold. Then smile and know that it is done.

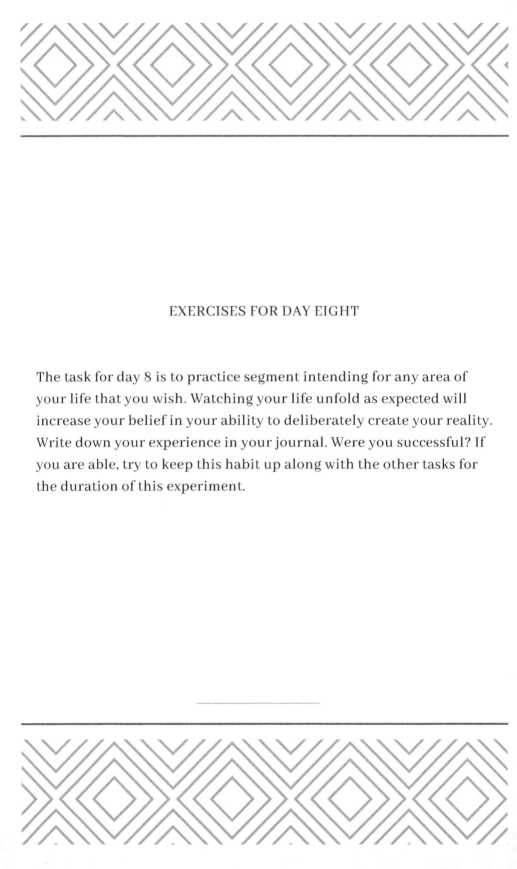

EXERCISES FOR DAY EIGHT

The task for day 8 is to practice segment intending for any area of your life that you wish. Watching your life unfold as expected will increase your belief in your ability to deliberately create your reality. Write down your experience in your journal. Were you successful? If you are able, try to keep this habit up along with the other tasks for the duration of this experiment.

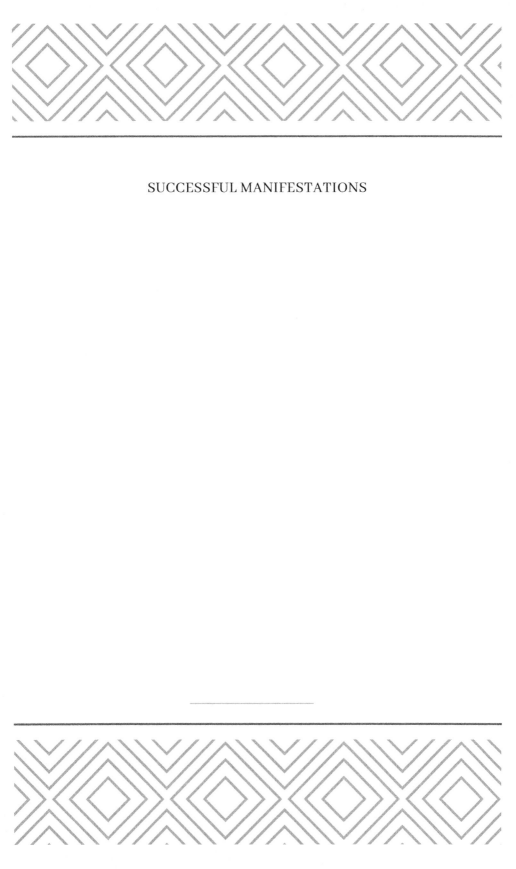

SUCCESSFUL MANIFESTATIONS

TO FIX A PROBLEM, IGNORE IT

So often we get caught up in seeing the negative aspects of situations (or our appearance) that they become all we see. It's easy to not like a physical trait, like your eyebrows, and look into the mirror and see the love child of Brook Shields and Groucho Marx staring back at you.....But so often we imagine others to be honed-in on our 'flaws', when really they cannot see them at all. I have a friend who is conventionally gorgeous and has been paid for acting, modelling and brand sponsorships. One day she told me that her eyes are different sizes. I immediately answered, "No, they're not" before even looking. But once I did look at her, it was all I could see! The one eye looked to be twice the size of the other and I exclaimed that she looked like a cubist painting. I had known her for years without ever seeing this trait, and I never would have seen it were she not to mention it. Now, I no longer see this 'flaw' given that some time has passed, but it is funny to reflect on.

EXERCISES FOR DAY NINE

Today's task is to ignore the problem. Yep, that's the task for day 9, to simply move on and let-go. Letting go is an important part of the manifestation process as it affirms your belief that you will receive what you have ask for. After all, you have asked the universe and what you want is on the way, there is no need to keep asking! If you want to change your nose, but love your eyes, put on some great eye-makeup that makes you feel confident. If you want to change your thighs but love your hair, style it and make it look great. Focus on the things that you already love about yourself and express some of that vibration-raising-self-love!

PRACTICE AN ATTITUDE OF GRATITUDE

Gratitude powers the Law of Attraction for so many reasons. One, it helps massively with confirmation bias. I mean, you are recounting all the other manifestations you created, thus affirming that the whole process works! Plus, you are raising your vibration, feeling good and are focusing on positive things, not the negative. Give thanks for all the amazing attributes you have. I find a powerful way to do this is when getting ready in the morning. You are already looking in the mirror, it is the perfect time for positive self-talk! You can definitely change attributes and enhance the way you look- you just don't need to, and the lack of 'need' will spur you there faster (not that you'll notice or care).

EXERCISES FOR DAY TEN

The exercise for day ten is similar to that of day nine. While yesterday's exercise had you play-up a physical attribute that you love, today's will have you journal all of the amazing physical qualities you already possess. In your journal or document, write down all the things you love about yourself. Don't be shy or modest! Give thanks for all the beauty you possess, and feel appreciative of it.

REASONS I AM BEAUTIFUL

LUCKY AND CHARMING

There are so many spells out there for how to increase your physical attractiveness with a 'glamour'. In much the same way that Superman was Clark Kent without glasses, a small change can completely change your look (to the point of being unrecognizable, apparently). A quick Google of beauty spells will reveal all sorts of rituals for changing your appearance with a magic spell. Whatever it is that you decide upon, don't look too closely into it. Of course, it should be safe and inexpensive, but the goal with finding a 'solution' is that you convince yourself that by undertaking this ritual or habit that you will bring about the change that you desire. And have fun with it! If you can power-up one of your lipsticks, or a favourite 'lucky shirt' and feel great about wearing it, you are not only convincing yourself that your desire is on the way, but you are improving your mood and becoming a vibrational match to your desire!

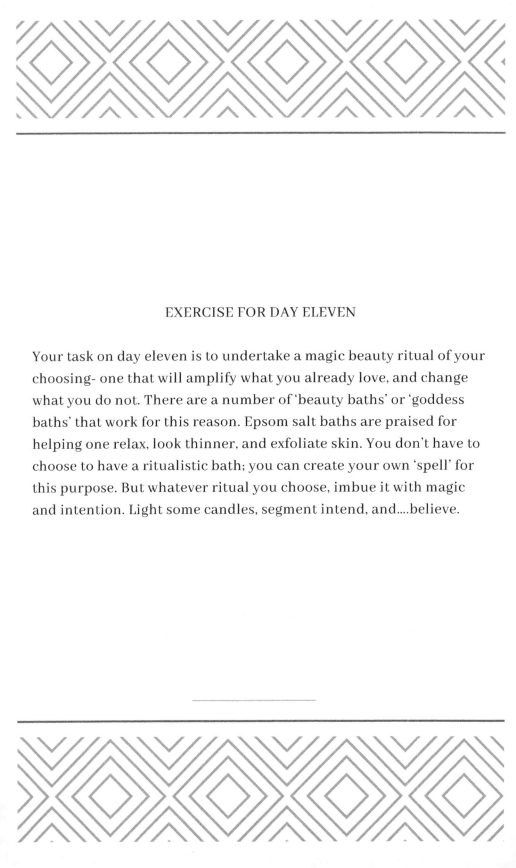

EXERCISE FOR DAY ELEVEN

Your task on day eleven is to undertake a magic beauty ritual of your choosing- one that will amplify what you already love, and change what you do not. There are a number of 'beauty baths' or 'goddess baths' that work for this reason. Epsom salt baths are praised for helping one relax, look thinner, and exfoliate skin. You don't have to choose to have a ritualistic bath; you can create your own 'spell' for this purpose. But whatever ritual you choose, imbue it with magic and intention. Light some candles, segment intend, and....believe.

SO LET IT BE WRITTEN, SO LET IT BE DONE

Scripting is a very powerful way of manifesting your desires. It is mentioned repeatedly in so many books and videos focused on Law of Attraction techniques. And there is a reason for this, it really does work. If you're not familiar with the concept of scripting, it is simply the process of journaling, with gratitude and excitement, from the position of your future-self. So much of what drives the Law of Attraction is feeling as if you have already obtained what it is that you want. Feeling the enjoyment and excitement of having lighter (or darker) hair, having longer eyelashes...whatever it is that you're after. To script, you will write in your journal the experience you have had since receiving your heart's desire. A great way to do this is to write a letter to a friend, describing how happy you are not that you have what you want, how excited you are, what it is that you are feeling and experiencing. You can do this exercise once or you can do it many times, it is up to you. Some people will create a magic 'box' in which they place their letters, and tell themselves that whatever they place in the box has and will come true. It really is like mailing a letter off to Santa!

EXERCISES FOR DAYS TWELVE THROUGH EIGHTEEN

You may script a letter from your future-self if you find that enjoyable. It can be an amazing way of clarifying how you wish to feel and all the reasons you are trying to manifest change. The act of repeatedly writing out an affirmation in the future tense is also very powerful. For the next seven days, engage in a "7 X 77" practice of scripting. This is a pretty famous technique, and is often done with the numbers 3X33 or 5X55. These are all auspicious numbers, although 7's are thought to be very lucky. In this scripting technique, you will write out one sentence that resonates with you. The key is to write it from your future self, and with joy and gratitude.

A very common way to state this is by beginning your sentence with "I am so happy and grateful now that..."

Perhaps you want longer hair? You might write out:

I am so happy and grateful now that my hair has grown out three inches." You will write this sentence out seventy-seven times in your journal, and will continue to write out this phase 77 times each day for the next week.

EXERCISES FOR DAYS TWELVE THROUGH EIGHTEEN

You may script a letter from your future-self if you find that enjoyable. It can be an amazing way of clarifying how you wish to feel and all the reasons you are trying to manifest change. The act of repeatedly writing out an affirmation in the future tense is also very powerful. For the next seven days, engage in a "7 X 77" practice of scripting. This is a pretty famous technique, and is often done with the numbers 3X33 or 5X55. These are all auspicious numbers, although 7's are thought to be very lucky. In this scripting technique, you will write out one sentence that resonates with you. The key is to write it from your future self, and with joy and gratitude.

A very common way to state this is by beginning your sentence with "I am so happy and grateful now that..."

Perhaps you want longer hair? You might write out:

I am so happy and grateful now that my hair has grown out three inches." You will write this sentence out seventy-seven times in your journal, and will continue to write out this phase 77 times each day for the next week.

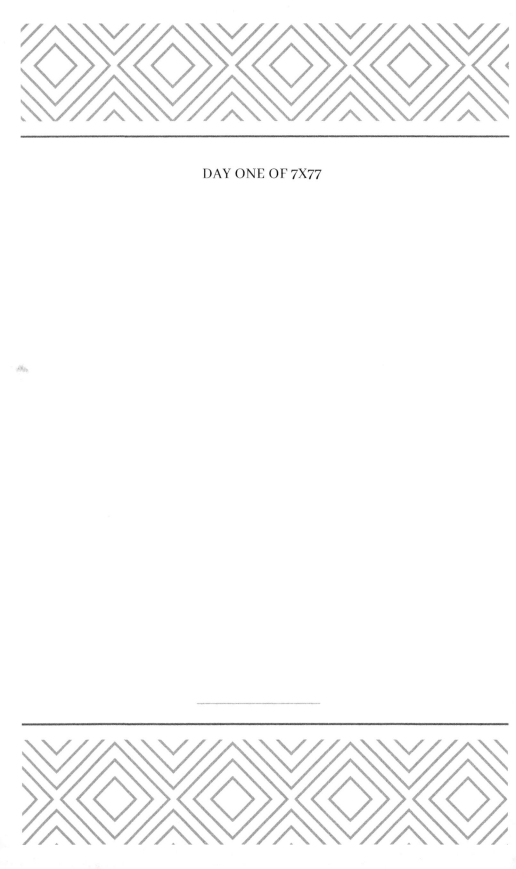

DAY ONE OF 7X77

DAY TWO OF 7X77

DAY THREE OF 7X77

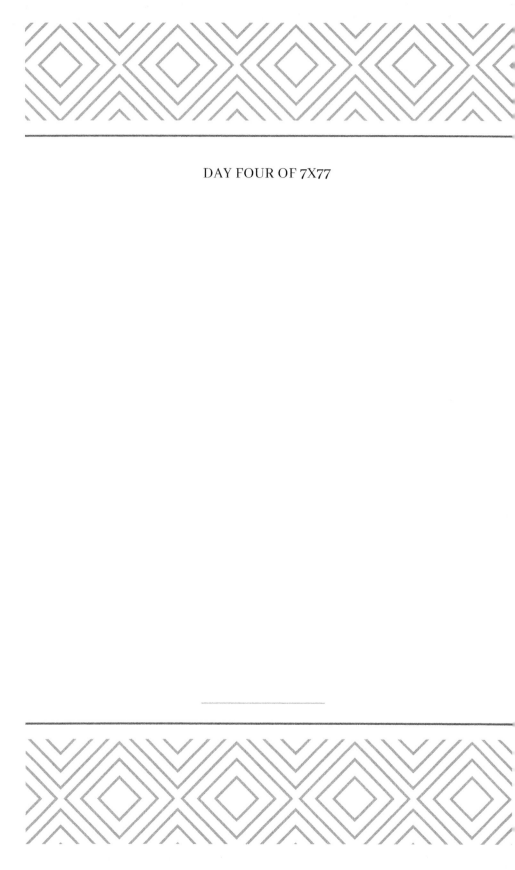

DAY FIVE OF 7X77

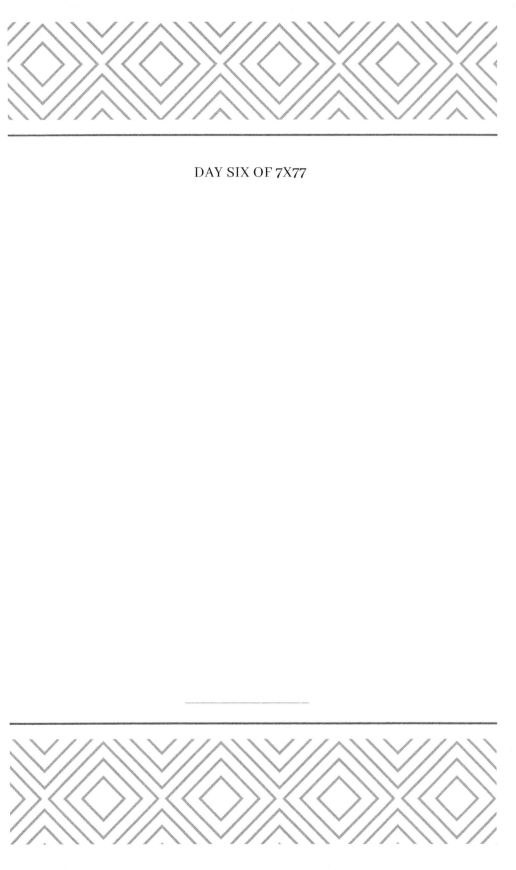

DAY SIX OF 7X77

DAY SEVEN OF 7X77

QUANTUM SORCERY

I read a book by Magnus Zea years ago called Quantum Sorcery that outlined what I thought was an ingenious strategy for becoming your future self. As mentioned, convincing yourself you are what you wish is a very important component of manifestation. Your subconscious mind has a hard time distinguishing between fantasy and reality. It really doesn't know the difference between a daydream and a memory. One of the manifestation tricks mentioned in this book is to create a fantasy space that you will come back to and visit each night before bed, in which things are visualized exactly as you desire. In this space you are to give yourself a new name, to drive home that this is a fantasy space, and imagine yourself looking as you wish. You can create whatever environment you feel most comfortable in, whether that is a castle, a modern loft or even a tree fort. But it is to be consistent, so that it becomes increasingly entrenched in your mind. When you go there in your mind before bed, envision yourself looking exactly as you want, and by visiting this space know that it will happen. It is the act of going to the magical place in your mind that creates the life you want. It is kind of like a mental vision board.

EXERCISE FOR DAY NINETEEN

You've made it all the way to day nineteen! Today's (or rather tonight's) task is to create this mental space where the new you that you have been envisioning can come to life. Go to this place before bed, knowing that it is only a matter of time before your dream vision becomes a reality. You can revisit this place nightly, even after this experiment has ended, and can tailor it to all sorts of manifestations!

DREAM IT POSSIBLE

Vision boards are an old-school staple of manifesting and are almost always mentioned when deliberate creation is being discussed. As the name suggests, vision boards are essentially a board full of images that represent your goals and dreams. A vision board is a very useful a tool for clarifying, maintaining and concentrating your focus on these goals. It's about making the ideas and dreams in your head more concrete.

 The goals can relate to any area of your life, but can of course relate to things you wish to change about your appearance. The idea is to feel inspired. If you put up a bunch of photos that may you feel uncomfortable or self-conscious, then the vision board it defeating its purpose. It is meant to make you feel joyful anticipation of the great things to come, not feel unhappy about where you're at.

DREAM IT POSSIBLE

A vision board serves three core purposes. The objectives of a vision board are:

To identify and clarify your goals – Visualizing your goals on a piece of board will make the goals more concrete. The purpose is to know exactly what success, confidence, attractiveness or happiness looks like to you.

To reinforce your daily affirmations – The purpose of a vision board is also to act as a daily reminder of your dreams. With a vision board, you create a visual representation of your goals and you are reminded about your goals every day.

To maintain focus on the wish – As well as reinforcing your daily affirmations, the purpose of a vision board is to help you maintain focus to avoid getting sidetracked or accepting less than you actually wanted.

Visualization is a powerful motivator. It's helpful to include affirmations on your vision board and use them to your advantage. If you can create a vision board that gives you hope and self-belief, you are on the right track.

DREAM IT POSSIBLE

You don't want to end up in a situation where your vision board is daunting and causes you to feel stressed out. The affirmations and the support you receive from the vision board is crucial for empowerment.

So, what is the best time to look at your vision board? You want to look at it either first thing in the morning or the last thing at night. Starting your day visualizing your goals can ensure you spend the whole day feeling great about these objectives without necessarily thinking too much about them.

On the other hand, just before bed is a good time to spend a few minutes reminding yourself of the dreams ahead of you and ensuring your sub-consciousness continues to think about these objectives while you sleep.

EXERCISES FOR DAY TWENTY

Today is day twenty, almost there! By now you should be feeling much better about what it is that you are trying to manifest, and have hopefully already begun to see (and feel) positive changes in your life. To continue the progress that you have made, create a vision board of what your new physique will look like, and place it somewhere it can be seen. You can create a digital vision board and place it as the background to your cell phone or computer, or can cut out several pictures that represent the new you. This vision board will continue to inspire belief after this experiment has ended, and to keep the positive momentum you have established flowing

CELEBRATE SUCCESS

We don't tend to achieve big life achievements in leaps and bounds. By including progress in your gratitude journal or scripting you are reminding yourself of the progress you are making, and affirming that you are no longer 'acting' as if but becoming who you want to be. If you notice positive changes, you speed up your progress and gain a lot of positive energy from your successes.

Celebrate Achievements

As you notice positive progress, take time to celebrate success. You don't need to buy yourself a gift for each step in the right direction, but you do want to take time to embrace successes. Small victories lead to big gains.

EXERCISE FOR DAY TWENTY-ONE

You have made it to the end of this experiment! Congratulate yourself for following through to the end! Record any successes you have had in your journal, and put it in a special place. This now acts as a 'book of proof' for your next manifestation project. To keep your vibration high, do something to celebrate this milestone. Turn on some music and dance, watch a great TV show, or meet-up with friends. And do so as the new person you were previously only 'acting as if' you were.

NOTEWORTHY MANIFESTATIONS

IT BEGAN WITH A SINGLE STEP...

The Law of Attraction always works, and whether or not it is working in our favor is a matter of personal choice. Learning how to consciously and deliberately create your reality is a process that takes time and effort. However, once you have improved upon these skills, it should become easier and easier to manifest positive changes into your life and into your appearance. I hope that you have found these exercises helpful, and will continue to refine your own creation process.